Phosphorescence

AF668400

Suganya Sundar

BookLeaf
Publishing

Presentation by *BookLeaf Publishing*

Web: www.bookleafpub.com

E-mail: info@bookleafpub.com

ISBN : 9789357210133

First edition 2022

DEDICATION

To all living out there who haven’t got a rock bottom to hit.

ACKNOWLEDGEMENT

I'm grateful for such an opportunity from Book leaf publishing. To all out there living and dead that shaped me into who I am today and to all who have directly or indirectly helped me .

PREFACE

Consider this a dare I have to myself to see if I'm gutsy enough to find out who I really am. Me minus all that I believe to be good and bad; all the quotations that inspire me and all the words of others that got to my head. A challenge of any size puts our own SWOT analysis into perspective.

Ingredients list.

Ingredients list
Lies between the label lines
All our healthy lives.

Birth.

Seed sown early fall
Soaked sprouted sprung up late spring
An eternal boon.

Art.

A hot iron box
Moving over crease of shirt
Loss of a rare art.

Panic!!

Red battery line
Panic!! hand reach for charger
Near the wilted plant.

Landscaping.

Little grey squirrel
Nibbling on swollen leaf buds
Nature's landscaper.

Moon bits.

A careful mother
Cutting nails of her baby
Waxing crescent moons.

Photo.

Still branches of trees
Midnight, deafening silence
Oh! A live picture.

Comma.

Swirling dry brown leaf
Fast, slow, lands befriending wind
Another journey.

Joy.

Shiny soap bubble
Floating towards a kid - Pop!!
A sweet giggling sound.

(A)theist.

(A)theist- the one
Whose thoughts are often with gods
For better and worse.

Freedom.

Leisure fondling breeze
Caress the dandelion
Freeing the pappus.

Shadow play.

Watch ! Through the window
Sun, cumulus clouds and wind
Divine shadow play.

Oxymoron.

A bright starry night
A live glimpse of history
Fine oxymoron.

Right of way.

A cautious squirrel
Crossing cold concrete road- Stop!
They have got the Green.

Balance.

Chaos's ecstasy
Discipline's melancholy
A cat on the wall.

Teaching.

The sun doesn't rise
The earth rotates towards east
An inconvenience.

Inevitable.

Wild beast and meek prey
Coexist; for its a rule
A concrete jungle.

Stress belly.

A big tough belly
Thought & called a glutton blind
Well played cortisol !

Timelapse.

A tree through seasons
Still - has leaves, sans leaves, new leaves.
Learn, unlearn, relearn.

Bibliophile.

Crouching from darkness
Glad everyone is asleep
A rat & a reader.

Dream.

Tapping a button
The World changes for better
Dreams are free of cost.

www.ingramcontent.com/pod-product-compliance
Lightning Source LLC
Chambersburg PA
CBHW062205160726
48282CB00027B/1010
9789357210133